Welcome!

"Why not go out on a limb? That's where the fruit is." If Mark Twain's observation is accurate, our artists are hanging off the limbs and filling their buckets full of fruit as they stretch their imagination and create completely unique and avant-garde projects. Just like a freestyle biker or skateboarder can pick his own moves for a show-stopping performance, our freestyle artists are doing their own thing to make projects that defy description. In *Freestyle*, we've set our artists free and allowed them to show their stuff. With techniques and projects that are a little on-the-edge, they show that it's okay to have your own style. Now go out on a limb and set your style free to create projects that show off your personality and profess who you are.

4 Chapter One
Looks Like an Ad

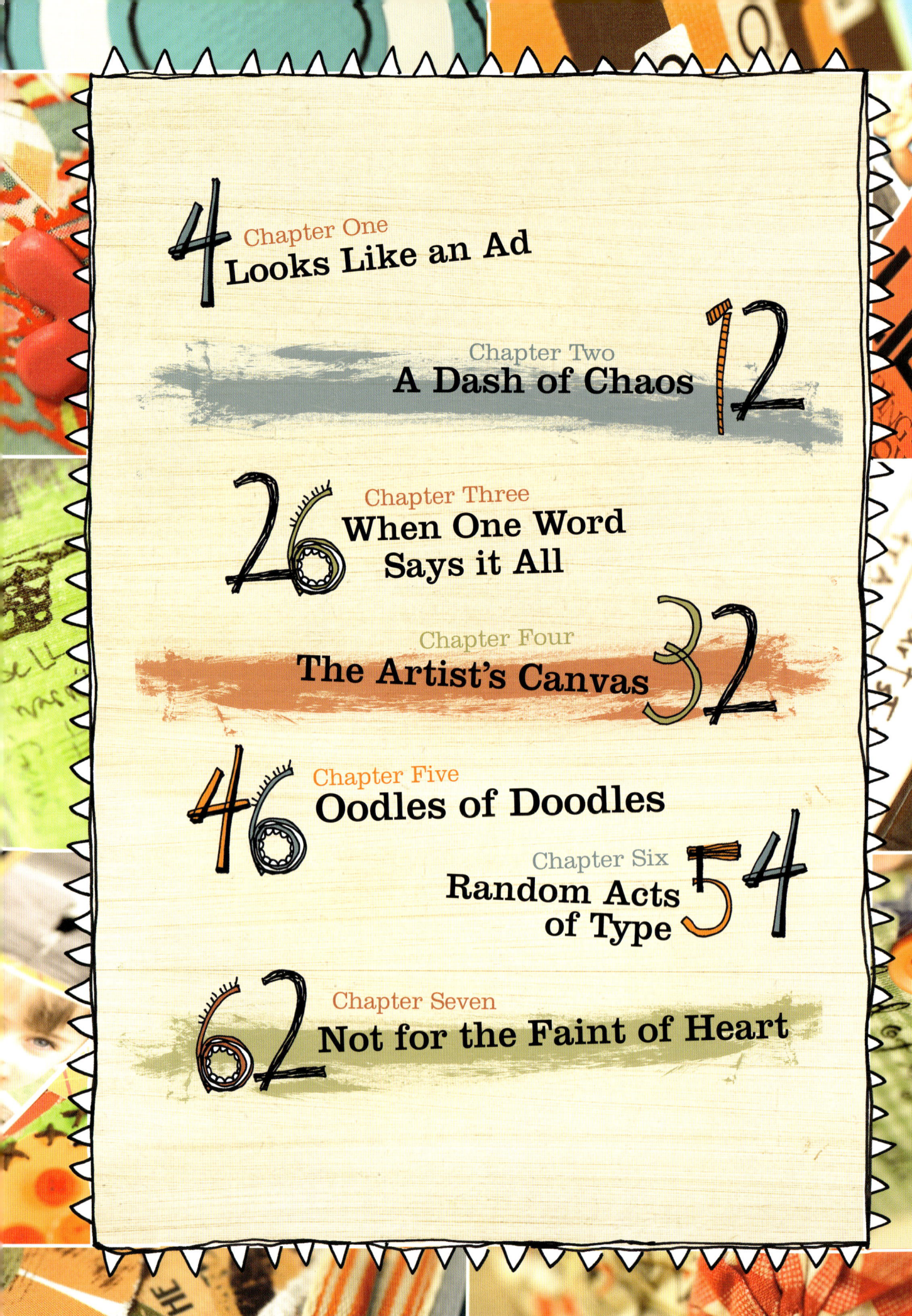

12 Chapter Two
A Dash of Chaos

26 Chapter Three
When One Word Says it All

32 Chapter Four
The Artist's Canvas

46 Chapter Five
Oodles of Doodles

54 Chapter Six
Random Acts of Type

62 Chapter Seven
Not for the Faint of Heart

Marilyn Healey

Rhonna Farrer

Jenn Bertsch

Ashley Wren

Danielle Thompson

Genevieve Simmonds

Ashley Calder

Kelli Crowe

Kim Henkel

Brenda-Mae Teo

Linda Albrecht

Zina Wright

Chris Ford

Emily Falconbridge

Tia Bennett

Séverine Di Giacomo

Erin Trimble

the artists of autumn leaves

CHAPTER **one**

Looks Like An Ad

Admit it. You have a magazine addiction. *Cosmo*, *People*, *Real Simple*, *Martha*. Whatever your favorite (or favorites), we know you like glancing through the pages, looking for new fashion trends, new recipes, new ways to decorate your boudoir or new ways to show off your freshly Botoxed lips. While you're looking for style inspiration, look for inspiration for your paper-art projects, too. Pay attention to the colors, design and typesetting for fresh ideas for your scrapbook pages. Let your layouts be as eye-catching as the ads that inspired them.

Hip Little Dude
By Danielle

Convert photos to grayscale and adjust the contrast using Curves. Digitally tint the stripes in the hat. Print onto textured blue cardstock. Rub blush-colored chalk onto cheeks. Silhouette the other two photos in Photoshop and print on darker blue cardstock. Use rub-ons to spruce up the photo and title.

Floppies
When I first started going to school, the only storage media we had available to us were floppy disks that held between 720 KB and 1.4 MB of data. One of my first portfolio pieces done in Director fit on a single floppy. It took me a week to make everything fit (there were no gifs or jpgs back then). If you wanted to transport a large file, you'd have to archive it in pieces, so you'd end up with 10 floppies for a single job.

Syquest
Syquest disks were a huge leap forward. Suddenly, you could store between 44 and 88 MB of data on a single disk. Granted, the disk was 5.5 x 5.5 inches and .5 inch thick, so you weren't exactly sticking them in your pocket, but you could fit an entire job on it and send it to the printers without archiving it into 10 pieces. When I worked at MicroCopy I used loads of these – and they were so big, we used a bad disk as a fob on our restroom key so people wouldn't lose it.

Zip Disks
My last year in school, these babies were introduced, and suddenly I had 100 MB of storage at my fingertips. I thought I was so slick, because I'd take my SCSI Zip drive into school with a copy of Mac System 7.0 on it, boot from the Zip drive, and be able to run the newest version of Adobe Photoshop (4.0) on the newest system software. I think that's when I started thinking like a geek, trying to outwit one of the three archaic LCIII's (with color monitors!) we had in our lab.

Jaz Disks
Jaz disks were introduced when I was working my first real job, at a skateboard company. Suddenly you jumped from 100 MB of data to 1 whole GB– 10x the storage capacity! I used to be able to fit an entire catalog on one of these bad boys. They also came as 2GB disks. Sadly, everything I ever did at the skateboard company was on a Jaz disk that I misplaced, so I lost all of the t-shirt designs, video intros, zines, ads, websites and catalogs I worked on while there.

CD & DVD-Rs
And then, the recordable CD rendered all of the previous media as dead as a dinosaur. Once upon a time, you had to pay a service bureau big bucks to burn a CD for you, and it was unreliable at best. I paid $10 each for every CD I made for portfolio reviewing, but three years out of school CD burners were standard on every computer, allowing you to store 650 MB of data on a wafer of plastic. And now, DVD-Rs let you store 4.7 GB of data on a similar platter.

A brief history of REMOVABLE STORAGE MEDIA in my career...

Geeks in the Future
By Chris

In Photoshop CS2, create a new 8¼"x 8¼" document. Use the line tool to draw a set of crop marks in, leaving ⅛" bleed around the document. This area allows you to trim your layout to 8"x 8" without any gaps in color along the edges. Use the Custom Shape tool to draw the boxes, talk balloon, rounded rectangles and female icon. Add photos, titles and journaling. Use a grunge brush to distress the entire layout. Reverse image and print onto t-shirt transfer paper. Iron image onto newsprint cardstock, then trim along crop marks.

Family Picnic
By Rhonna

In Photoshop CS2, select the photo filter and heighten the sepia coloring for the larger photo. Crop the photo to focus on a part of the larger photo, and apply an "underwater" photo filter. Using brushes, create a fun, retro feel in various colors. Create the diamond shape using Custom Shapes. Add text and journaling.

1950's family picnics~making biscuits with aprons, cowboy hats, gold medal~ looks like an old vintage ad; cooking together, father & son, out in nature, amoung family. thank goodness for grandpa, our faithful photographer

Why is She Smiling?
By Marilyn

Arrange photo and papers for background. Apply a sundial rubbing on vellum. Add hand-cut title to vellum rubbing. Use hole-reinforcers as stencils. Color some of the reinforcers and add to page. Sew beads onto page. Back a bookplate with paper, a reinforcer and a bead, then stitch to layout.

Myopie
By Severine

Print two images in the same photo using a photo editor. Divide the layout in thirds, using paper strips as dividers.

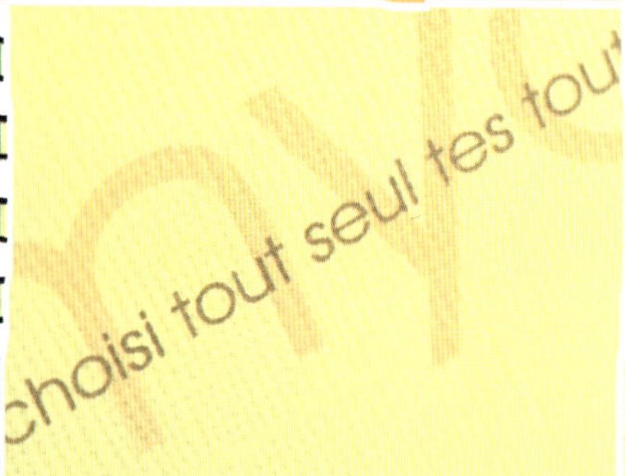

Space
By Brenda-Mae

Print journaling directly onto photo. Sand edges. Apply rub-ons and a strip of patterned paper.

Vintage Chic
By Linda

Create background with assorted papers. Print title onto transparency. Hand color the back side of the letters with markers and highlight the edges of the letters on the front with a white paint pen. Attach to layout. Hand cut foam images and stamp with acrylic paint.

06-25-04
By Ashley W.

Place extra large number stickers on cardstock. Using a small ink pad, generously dab around the number stickers. When dry, gently remove the stickers. Place two pictures underneath the masked numbers and tape the corners with masking tape. Embellish with stickers, paper flower and tag with journaling.

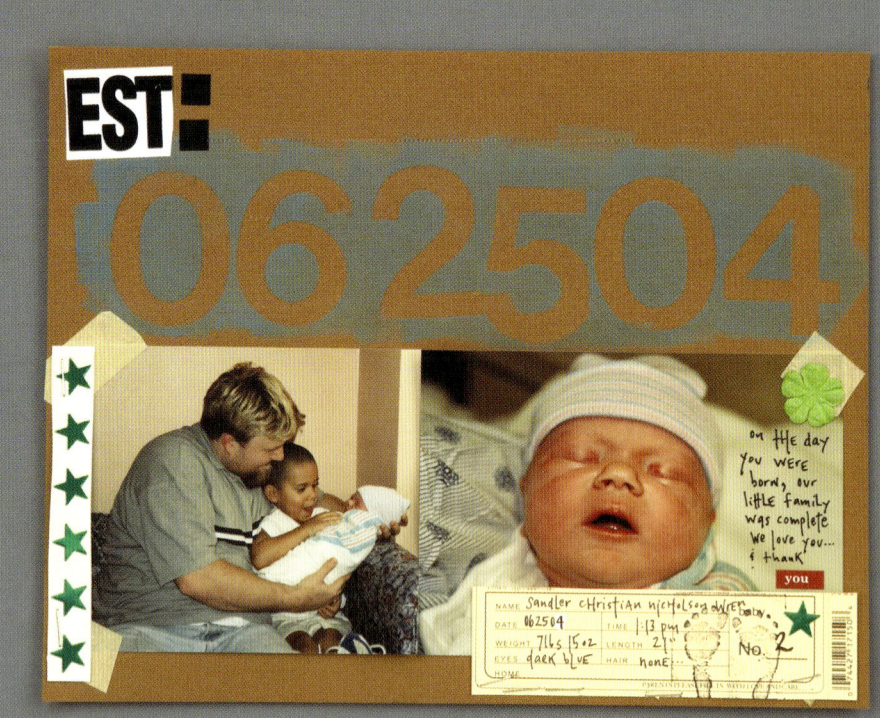

A Little Push
By Tia

Manipulate photo on the computer and remove most of the background with an eraser tool. Print photo onto a transparency and layer over paper.

My Hope
By Brenda-Mae

Ethan and Hannah, children of my only and dearest sister, you have brought much joy and delight into our hearts. My hope for you is that as you begin to increase in understanding and take hold of the plans and purposes of God in your lives, you will be consumed with a love and a passion for Him and the work His Kingdom. May His truth be the light that guides your journey through life.

my ★ hope

To create the text circles (on the photo), open a photo in a graphics-editing program. Draw large circular paths around the faces of the subjects in the photo. Using the text tool, type the names of the subjects onto the circular path in white. Reduce the opacity to 40%.

CHAPTER **two**

A Dash of Chaos

"A creative mess is better than a tidy void." Doesn't a messy workspace mean that a creative genius has been at work? Of course it does! Our artists wholeheartedly agree, and they even translate the same notion to their works of art. They have thrown out the templates and blueprints, have forgotten about lining things up and are letting things fall where they may. Here you'll see a little messy, a little chaotic and a lot of fun. So leave the mess and let your creative muse come out to play!

This Baby
By Ashley C.

wounded solider galloping crawl

sweetest baby voice babbling chorus of mumma mumma mumma, smiling round face she pulls herself to standing, peering up past my knees delicate baby kisses, dusty cookie lips,

this baby makes my heart happy.

To make white tissue flower, cut three flowers from white tissue paper. Stitch layers together in the center, adding small white beads. Trace second flower shape on layout where white tissue flower will be adhered. Hand stitch around edges, adding green beads in some of the stitches. Adhere white tissue flower over center of embroidered flower. To make the green flower, layer six pieces of green tissue. Trim into circle using small scallop-edge scissors. Stitch layers together and add a clear button to the center.

Groucho Max
By Kelli

Cut flower petals from cardstock and arrange on background. Use an X-Acto knife to cut around a couple petals, forming small photo corners.

Their Light Within
By Danielle

Manipulate a butterfly image in Photoshop. Adjust the contrast with Levels and apply a Cutout Artistic Filter to the image. Make image blue and print out. Cut out image, including some shapes within the butterfly. Back the openings with patterned paper. Adhere butterfly to the page with 3-D adhesive dots. Hand draw decorative elements on and around the butterfly and woman. Chalk on some areas of the layout.

Beginner's Mind
By Ashley C.

Cut a large piece of muslin -- large enough to cover the page plus two inches on each side. Coat with gesso and let dry. Cover plain cardstock with fabric; wrap extra fabric to back and secure. Lightly pencil in patterns, then outline with black permanent ink. When dry, paint fabric with watercolors. Draw heart outline on tag and machine stitch. Layer notebook paper, solid colored paper and corrugated cardboard together and stitch around edge.

Pink House
By Kim

Tear muslin to 10"x14". Fold in half, leaving two inches on the bottom for the fabric scallops. Cut different size wool scallops and circles. Using embroidery floss, hand stitch scallops and circles to bottom of muslin. Stitch buttons on the circles and stitch bows over scallops. Hand stitch fabric to cardstock. Include journaling and a stamped image on a small piece of folded cardstock.

I Have This Hat...
By Kelli

Cut flower petals from ribbon. Fray the edges, then coat with Fray Check. Stitch each petal to the page. Make a small hole in the middle of the flowers, then run knotted ribbon through the hole. Secure paper-covered floral wire to the page with fine gauge wire that loops around and ties on the back of the page.

Sabor
By Chris

Scan memorabilia and extract from background. Scan cardboard. Arrange memorabilia and photos on top of cardboard layer. Assemble photo collage. Add photos to negative frames and slide holders. Scan and add titles and phrases from magazines. Duplicate fire photo, placing it in front of type layer. Apply a Layer Mask, and use a soft-edged brush to mask out everything but the flame. Set the layer mode to Multiply so the flame appears to be circling the title.

Good Friends By Ashley C.

Arrange blocks of inked patterned paper over embossed background paper. Machine stitch swirls along the page. Layer photos over stitching. Reverse print flower dingbats onto the backside of patterned paper and cut out. Cut out one large flower from patterned paper and mat with a second patterned paper. Trim excess paper from backing around edges of flower. Hand letter title, names and date inside petals. Journal on photos with a white pen.

Sand and Sun
By Danielle

Arrange photos in Photoshop. Create layers of sun "rays" on top of the largest photo and give them different opacities so you can see the photo through them. Extend the "rays" on the large photo onto the page with strips of cardstock. Hand cut ocean waves and add hand stitching.

What If
By Rhonna

In Photoshop CS2, open photo, adjust the Curves, Levels and Hue & Saturation. Print on photo paper and adhere to cardstock. Use a custom brush and print out the brush onto inkjet transparency. Cut out and adhere to layout. Use paints to add color in layers. Add epoxies, die cut flowers, rub-ons and sticker flowers.

My Favorite Little Ones
By Kim

Tear a piece of muslin to cover cardstock. Make flowers from pipe cleaners and stitch to muslin. Hand stitch fabric to cardstock. Stamp title and hand write journaling; stitch to fabric. Mat small photos on cardstock and write names on mat. Punch hole and add loopy brad. Color over journaling with colored pencils. Randomly tie matted photos to flowers using embroidery floss.

Reach for the Stars
By Danielle

Convert the large photo to grayscale and adjust the contrast with Curves. Do the same with other two photos, but make them duotones of aqua and navy and pink and navy. Adhere to layout and add ribbon on the diagonal. Cut out stamped stars and adhere with foam tape, adding sequin stars around them. Apply rub-ons to spell "Reach" and fill in with chalk.

Napa Style
By Jenn

Back acrylic letters with book paper. Make swirl designs with buttons.

AG
By Kelli

Punch circles and trim by hand to give a less finished look. Adhere to layout with foam tape. Edge circles with white paint and a fine-tip paintbrush. Draw a curvy line around photo and use as a guide for journaling.

Feeling Blessed
By Emily

Dye a piece of paper towel in gold ink. When dry, adhere to pink cardstock. Use henna tattoo stencil as a mask with pink spray paint. Cut fabric heart and attach, adding painted wings with a wing stamp. Punch holes down the side of the page and weave with ribbon strips.

I Love You
By Zina

Use a coaster for the flower center and for the journaling. Stitch around pillow chips to make the petals. Paint chipboard letters and use them as the stem.

10 By Severine

Paint a dot circle with acrylic paint. Punch circles from different papers and decorate them with black embellishments.

Minnie Kay
By Ashley C.

Layer paper, handkerchief, lace, trim and photo. Lightly tack down items with a glue stick. Lightly sketch out swirls and sew over the top, layering three or four rows of stitching. Create flowers from various items such as fabric, metal and paper with a button center.

Kaleidoscope
By Kim

Cut various sizes of irregular-shaped rings from cardstock. Glue to bottom left corner of background. Add a small strip of cardstock around edges of background. Ink color on a tag and use for journaling; tape tag to background. Include photos in an envelope attached to page.

CHAPTER three
When One Word Says It All

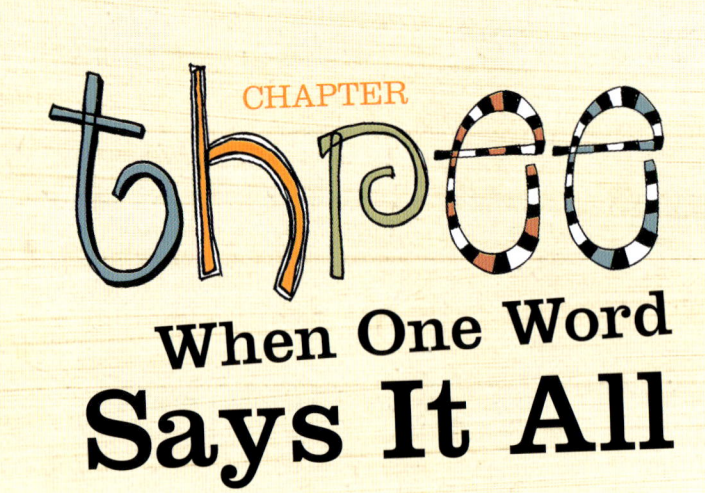

Moms are skilled at using only one word to get their point across. "Stop," "Now," "Enough," and "Quiet" are all one-word sentences that are understood by children and even spouses. Many times one word is enough to say it all. Sometimes it's enough to say it all on a layout. Putting only one word on a page allows you to focus on that word and try several funky techniques to make it stand out. "Come" and learn from these artists as they take their communication skills from home to their scrapbook pages and use one word to make a statement.

Wreckage
By Marilyn

Stamp title with paint. For left side, ink over a piece of mesh and color in a few holes with a colored pencil. Attach mesh to right side with staples and fold journaling strips over the edge.

Believe
By Rhonna

In Photoshop CS2, open photo, adjust the Curves, Levels and Hue/Saturation. Add patterned papers and photo frame from digital kits. Use dingbats for swirls, then add a Gradient Map to the swirl and title. Apply a Color Dodge to the large middle swirl. Use a stitching brush to add the stitching doodles with a Wacom Tablet. With Custom Shapes, create butterflies in various colors and sizes. For title and journaling, add a "rise" warp; add an edge brush for flair.

Foundations
By Linda

Collage papers on background. Print title letters onto canvas and hand cut individual letters; machine stitch randomly. Attach photos to layout and attach title with staples, rhinestone brads and star brads.

Comfort
By Jenn

Use miscellaneous items and photos to describe what a word means to you. Hand stitch around the cardstock.

29

Spooky
By Marilyn
Arrange photos on patterned paper. Print journaling onto a narrow strip of orange patterned paper. Cut stars from fun foam and adhere the cutouts and negative images to the layout. Back the negative images with book paper. Use a star cutout as a stamp and stamp with green paint. Use random letters to form title. Layer over vellum that has been cut out to look like fog.

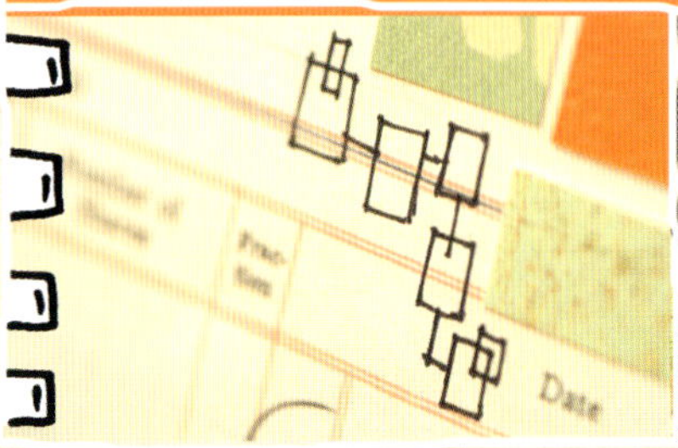

Panic
By Genevieve
Adhere bits and pieces of patterned paper and cardstock to background. Print title and journaling on patterned paper. Add a few doodles for embellishments.

Essence
By Linda

Paint corrugated cardboard for page border and title. Print title onto transparency and hand draw stars, then layer over cardboard piece. Layer pieces of transparency onto patterned paper strips and hand draw stars. Add buttons and snaps. Hand stitch along bottom border, on edges of the title block and on select photo edges.

Brothers
By Zina

Cut title and hearts from patterned paper. Ink the edges of the hearts and mat the title letters. Apply both to layout with foam tape.

31

CHAPTER

The Artist's Canvas

Picasso observed, "Every child is an artist. The problem is how to remain an artist once we grow up." Our artists must be smarter than Picasso because they seem to have figured it out. With everything from paint, color washes and watercolors to gesso, ink and Photoshop, these creative geniuses have added color to their pages and created customized backgrounds and paper. So put on your smock and play a while to see what innovative handiwork you can fashion.

Turning Five
By Marilyn

Print journaling in a tall, curved column. Print photo twice - once in purple and once in color. Cut the purple into strips and the color one into a circle. Adhere strips to page, then write large, expressive words in cursive with a colored pencil. Add journaling strip, photo and buttons. Adhere candy wrappers with purple eyelets. Hand stitch one large stitch in between some of the journaling.

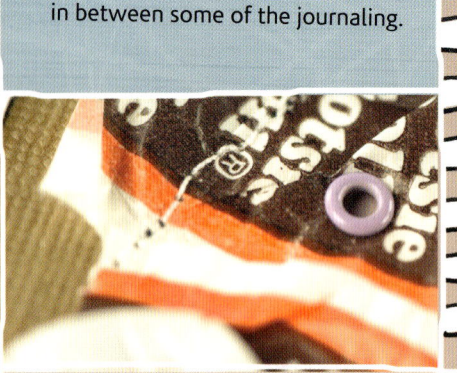

Summer Lily
By Ashley C.

Color wash dictionary pages to match layout. Cut letters from white felt. Add decorative stitching. Layer several pieces of fabric slightly larger than desired size for flower and sew button to middle. Trim around button. Cut from outer edge to the center, moving around the edge, fringing layers of fabric. Dampen and pull gently on petals to fray edges. Let dry and fluff. Use printed twill as stems.

Alex '05
By Kelli

Cut paper and extra photos into trapezoids. Sand and ink all the edges. Use rub-ons for the title.

It's All About the Love
By Marilyn

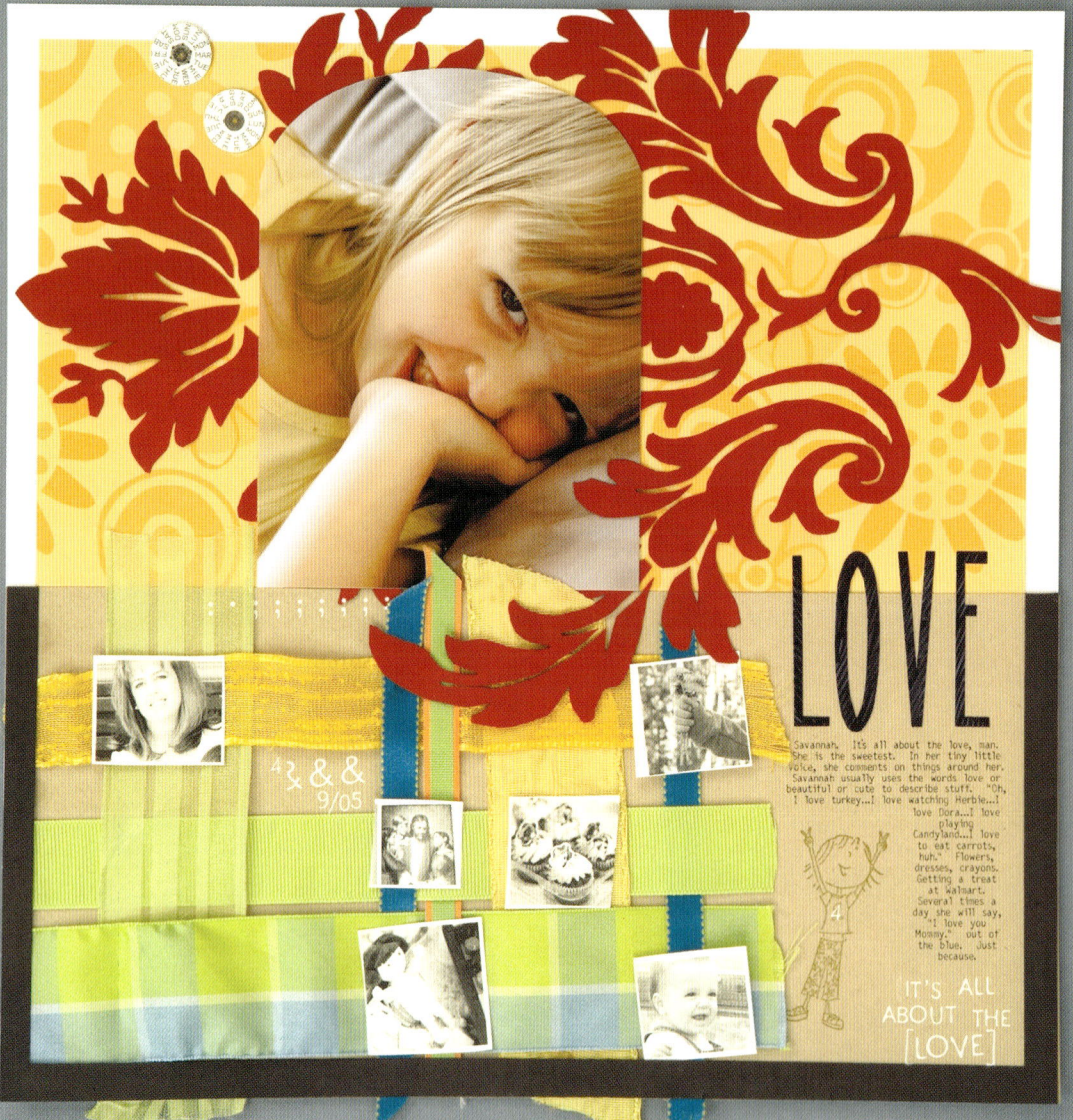

Cut a large design from red paper and secure to top of page. Add photo and watch parts. Print journaling onto kraft cardstock. Weave different ribbons on the bottom left corner. Add small photos on top.

He's So Silly
By Zina

Scan three patterned papers, then print onto a transparency. Cut the heart, border and circles from the transparencies. Cover the two outer photos with a patterned transparency.

Cheerio
By Jenn

Embellish cardstock with stitched flower rub-ons. Cut out and adhere around photo along with buttons. Cut slits at the top of layout and slide ribbon through. Adhere cardstock strips to layout; apply stitching rub-ons. Add photo and chipboard letters to layout.

Prepare
By Rhonna

In Photoshop CS2, open photo and desaturate it. Add magenta filter for the colored effects. Use various colored brushes at varying levels of opacity. Use a custom "hand quote" brush and color in to make the title.

Pink
By Brenda-Mae

To make the colored background for the journaling, color the whole background with watercolor pencils. Go over it with a damp paintbrush to create a watercolor effect.

Love
By Ashley C.

Stitch together wide strips of kraft cardstock. Cut lumpy circles from gesso-painted muslin, then paint with watercolors. Add lumpy scallop-edge circle to bottom of flower and set with button tied with string. Add string stems and muslin leaf. Layer fabric and paper under photo and stitch in place. Hand cut title from notebook paper, layer over paper and stitch through each letter.

Friendship
By Linda

Paint cardstock with light mustard-colored acrylic paint. Apply white paint to a piece of corrugated cardboard and "stamp" onto page to create the horizontal lines. Cut petal shape from rubber that is used as a cushion for rubber stamps to create large flowers. Use a socket tool to stamp round images with square holes. When dry, dry brush over all images with white paint.

2 Guys and a Girl
By Tia

Wipe textured cardstock with colored ink pads to create a background.

Gamers
By Danielle
To create patterned paper in Photoshop (right-hand page), create bars of different shades of yellow in the background. Layer lines of yellow text in different sizes and opacities. Layer photos on top of that, but allow the text and yellow bars to show through. Make the photos a subtle gray and adjust the Curves. Print onto white cardstock. Complete layout with photos and circle stamps.

Miss Lilly
By Kim
Tear fabric to 12"x10 ½". Use stencil, paint and a stippling brush to paint designs on fabric. Randomly hand stitch "X"'s and lines on fabric, adding buttons, notions, fabric and yoyos. Attach fabric to background with paper clips and metal clips. Tie twill and rickrack to clips and add decorative felt to one of the clips. Add title and journaling to cardstock circle.

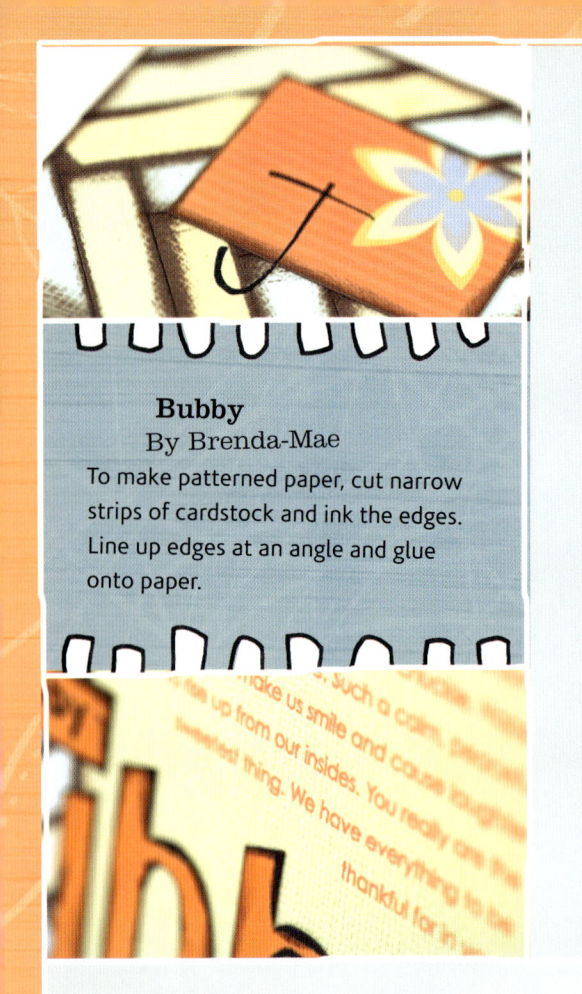

Bubby
By Brenda-Mae
To make patterned paper, cut narrow strips of cardstock and ink the edges. Line up edges at an angle and glue onto paper.

Fatherhood
By Zina
Cut out a shape from cardstock. Using it as a pattern, trace shape onto green cardstock. Paint in pattern with masking fluid. When dry, paint entire page with blue paint, painting right over masked pattern. When dry, gently peel off masking fluid, creating custom patterned paper. Add punched hearts to the design.

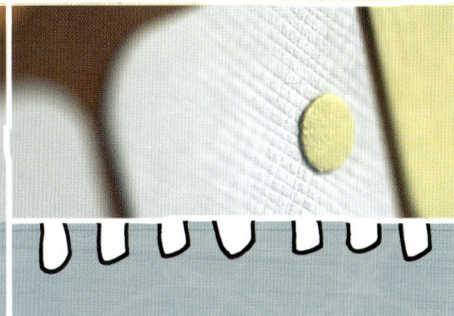

Le Petit Monde de Loan
By Severine

Cut several squares from cardstock and round the corners. Punch small circles from the same colors and adhere them to the squares. Create the title with overlapping text boxes.

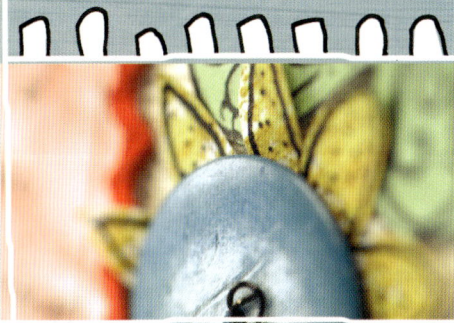

Barcelona
By Ashley C.

Paint corrugated cardboard with orange paint. Mix watercolors with a gel medium, roll brayer in paint and then transfer paint to torn notebook paper. Stamp harlequin pattern onto fabric with acrylic paint. When dry, age with walnut ink. Print or paint swirls onto kraft cardstock; cut out. Assemble all items along with photos. Add hand-cut title and draw swirls with permanent ink. Paint cardstock circle with watercolors and add journaling and rickrack.

Heart of a Sutta
By Ashley C.

Draw hearts, diamonds and dots on plain cardstock with permanent ink. Paint in with watercolors. Tear edge off heart patterned sheet and arrange on kraft cardstock. Stitch around edges. Layer white flannel, notebook paper, kraft cardstock and lace behind photo. Sew buttons in place, journal on cardstock and add title on small round tag with scalloped edge. Tie measuring tape and secure across bottom of photo.

Just One Normal Picture
By Kelli

For the background, hand cut circle frames. Lightly tape one third of the circles to the page. Brush and splatter blue paint over each circle with strips of paper. Let dry. Without removing any circles, layer the next one third of the frames. Paint over these with green paint and let dry. Repeat one last time with the white. When dry, remove the paper circles to reveal the negative space beneath.

Card Set
By Emily

Fold watercolor paper into cards. Paint with watered-down acrylics, creating a wash-like effect. While paint is still wet, draw or sketch into it with a lead pencil.

CHAPTER **five**

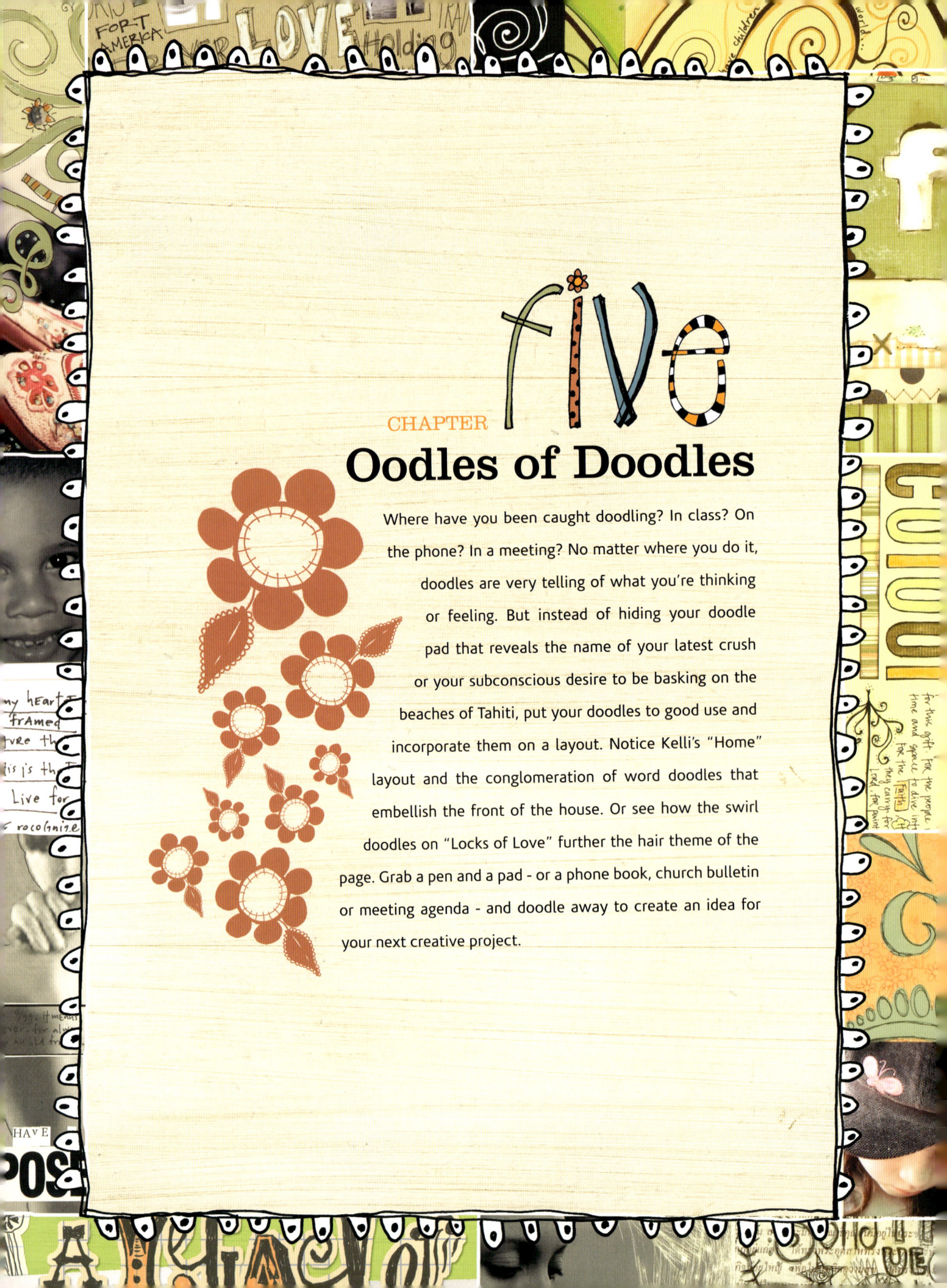

Oodles of Doodles

Where have you been caught doodling? In class? On the phone? In a meeting? No matter where you do it, doodles are very telling of what you're thinking or feeling. But instead of hiding your doodle pad that reveals the name of your latest crush or your subconscious desire to be basking on the beaches of Tahiti, put your doodles to good use and incorporate them on a layout. Notice Kelli's "Home" layout and the conglomeration of word doodles that embellish the front of the house. Or see how the swirl doodles on "Locks of Love" further the hair theme of the page. Grab a pen and a pad - or a phone book, church bulletin or meeting agenda - and doodle away to create an idea for your next creative project.

47

Home
    By Kelli

Draw the basic shapes for the page. Use an X-Acto knife to cut out all but the left side of the house so it opens. Paint the background and write "home" words on house. Fill a piece of cardstock with photos and place behind the flap. Add a ribbon chimney that doubles as a tab to open the flap.

Locks of Love
By Danielle

Hand draw a large heart in the middle of the connected pages, then adhere photos. Freehand swirls, hearts, journaling and title with pens to add meaningful interest to the layout.

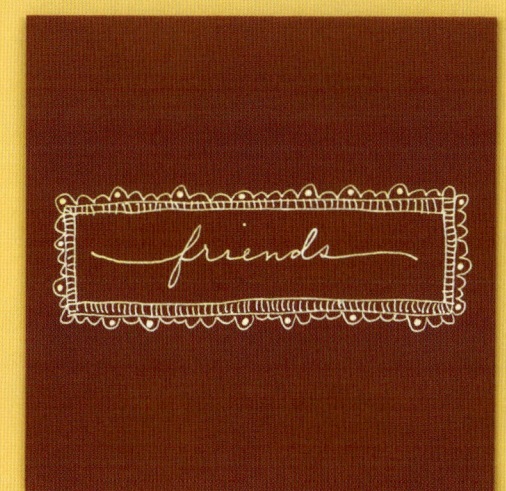

Doodle Cards
By Tia

Hand draw doodles on cards or get help from rubber stamps and computer images.

Best Friends
By Linda

Collage papers for background. For the border pieces, put right sides together, then turn over edges to the back, making folds at each corner. Paint the chipboard letter and cover the outer chipboard piece with paper, then attach photo corners. Have child write names and phrase, then hand stitch over the top.

Life in Colour
By Brenda-Mae

Draw frame and swirls in pencil, then go over in pen. To make the title ("colour"), print word onto cardstock and cut out letters. Using negative cutout as a stencil, place over cardstock and draw letters. Color in with watercolor pencils and go over with a damp brush. Outline letters with black pen.

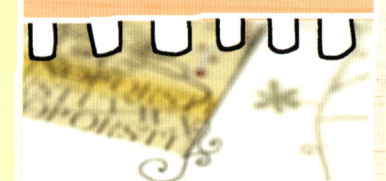

Step Daughter
By Zina
Draw swirls and title on cardstock, then cut out. Color in the title with watercolor pencils. Hand stitch swirls on the bottom part of the layout.

Stay True
By Emily
Collage book paper and scraps of paper to background. Adhere with gel medium, then apply coat of gel medium all over the top. When dry, doodle all over with a marker or pen. Sand a photo and attach to layout when dry.

Good Times
By Chris

Use Photoshop CS2 to lay a brushstroke overlay on top of a green background. Using Edit >> Fill, make the brushstrokes a slightly darker green than the background. Make sure Preserve Transparency is checked. Use a Wacom tablet to trace the title after you set it. Do the same for the dingbats used as doodles. Create a magic marker effect when filling certain letters in by checking Wet Edges in the brushes palette before painting them in. Use the Pen tool to draw rough shapes around all letters in title and dingbats. Make path a selection, then paste graph paper pattern into selection. Add distressing and drop shadow. Place photos and add drop shadows. Add journaling, then use the Transform tool to tilt the text block.

Purpose
By Ashley W.

Print a black and white photo onto textured cardstock. Sketch around the outlines of the photo with a pencil and a pen. Draw images onto the photo. Apply the negatives of label stickers near the drawings; journal inside them. Paint messily around the edges of cardstock.

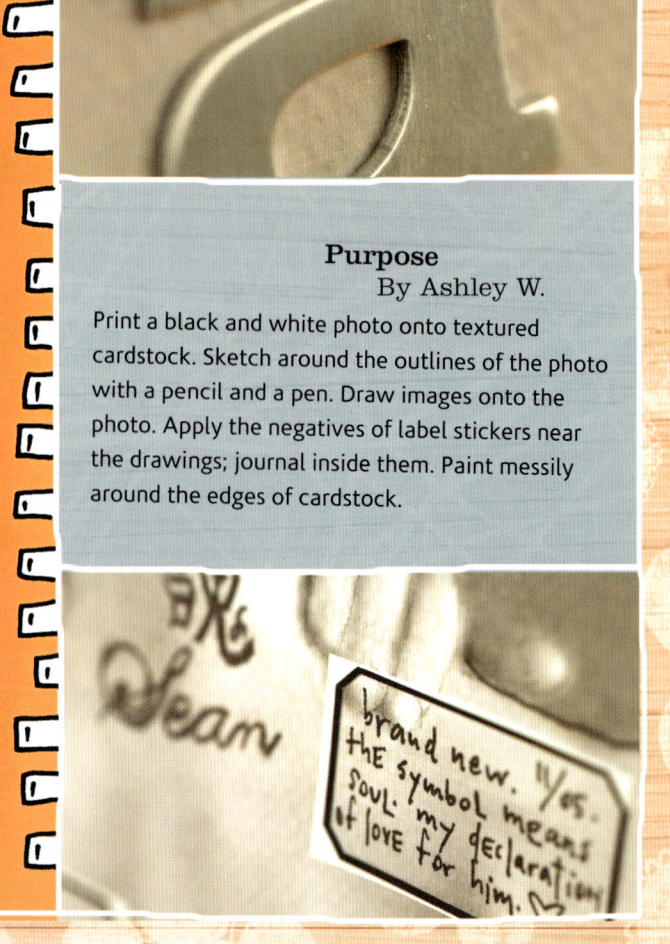

This One Picture
By Ashley W.

Ink edges of cardstock. Draw lines, then hand write journaling on the lines. Lightly draw a heart in pencil underneath the journaling. Apply rub-on wings and apply sequined ribbon over the pencil outline. Fill the heart with eyelets, brads, rhinestones, snaps and buttons. Staple rickrack to page.

Shoes
By Rhonna

To add color to a black and white photo, open photo, duplicate layer and desaturate. On black and white photo layer, select eraser at 100% and erase the part you don't want to be black and white. This will bring the colored photo from behind. Flatten image when finished. Print onto photo paper and adhere to layout, adding paint, sequins, glitter and doodles.

CHAPTER **Six**

Random Acts of Type

We paper artists have a lot of addictions. One of them - besides magazines - is fonts. This addiction is not so bad, however. Type plays an important part on every scrapbook page. The font you choose can add to the feeling you're trying to portray, and a mixture of fonts adds visual pleasure. Join these addicts as they play with fonts and even their own handwriting to add a little spunk and personality to their artwork.

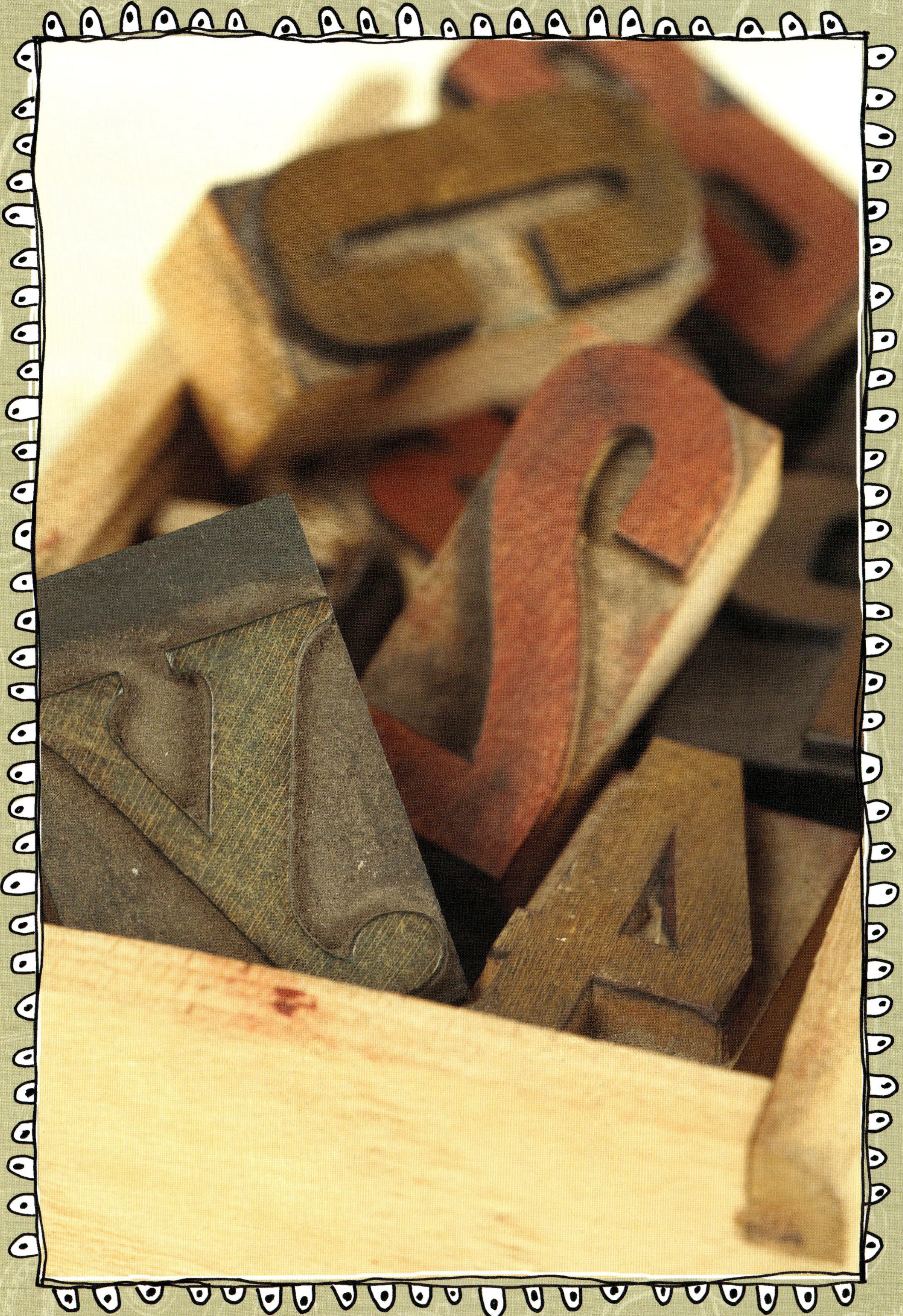

Brown Eyed Girl
By Rhonna

In Photoshop CS2, open photo, go to hue/saturation and desaturate photo. This will be your large photo. Adjust the opacity for a subtle vellum look. For the smaller photo, use the magnetic lasso tool to cut out the body. Adjust curves and hue/saturation, and apply the film grain filter. On separate layers of the text and brushes, apply the gradient map layer style to give this look. Finally, on the top layer, select black brushes and overlay light mode to achieve this burnt look.

Completion of the Sixth Grade
By Marilyn

For the journaling on the right side, make a colored text box with clear text, allowing the white paper to show through. Collage old book paper on the background and add photo on top.

Photographer's Paradise
By Kim

Hand stitch an "H" onto muslin. Stitch to page along with striped fabric. Heat emboss image on patterned paper. Add a fastener to top of embossed paper, including photo strips in the fastener. Write title on notebook paper; attach to layout with pink masking tape.

Two is Better
By Brenda-Mae

Layer text to create interest. Reduce opacity of the text ("1" and "2") to create a watermark effect. Use different fonts for added effect.

and on the day she was born she reached out and touched Her thumb, HEART in HAND as if to say, sister, i know you. it was the start of love

Heart in Hand
By Ashley C.
Cut 1" strips of several patterned papers. Ink edges and adhere to cardstock. Stitch heart and swirls onto background and sprinkle sequins around page. Add photo. Create an image the size of the entire layout and format journaling. Reverse print words on the back of patterned paper and cut out each word as a single piece. Ink edges with a large brush marker.

Lucky
By Ashley W.
Stamp polka dots randomly on patterned paper. Apply photos and adhere a paper clover over the top. Staple ribbon across page and apply rub-ons for the title; journal inside each letter.

Kim
By Severine

Create text in a photo editor. Mix the font size, color and direction.

Simple Pleasures
By Zina

Print "simple" onto paper; cut out. Adhere letters to photo with repositionable tape, then cut the word out of the photo. Back with patterned paper. Outline with a gel pen.

59

The Boys
By Kelli
Write words on photos with a fine-point pen. Embellish each word by making the lines thicker or colored. Make a border from small squares cut from paper and photos. Raise some of the squares with foam tape.

The Woods
By Tia
Print text directly on a photo by layering the photo behind the text. Cut out title printed in an intricate font.

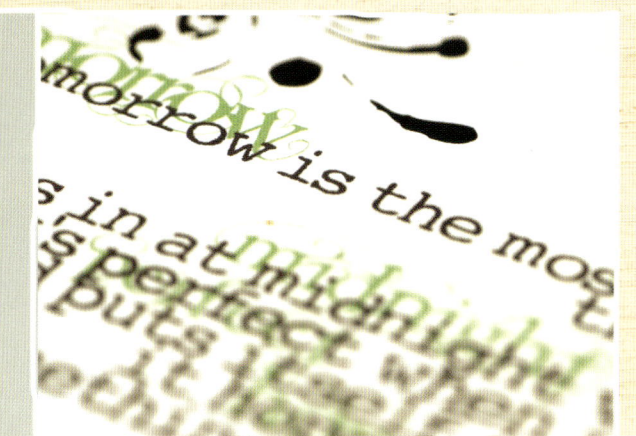

Tomorrow
By Genevieve

In Illustrator, fill a "J" with bright blue and lay text over the top. Make keywords green. Print, then cut out with an X-Acto knife.

I Will Not Change
By Chris

Scan a piece of rough-sawn cedar to use as a background. Using Photoshop CS2, add a yellow acrylic paint overlay using the Multiply Blend Mode, as well as a white overlay set to Normal. Add colored paint splashes and set title. Scan Polaroid photo mount and paste photo on top, setting blend to Multiply so mount shows through. Set type on photo, make it a selection, hide it and use the Layer Mask feature to cut the journaling out of the photo, so mount appears inside letters.

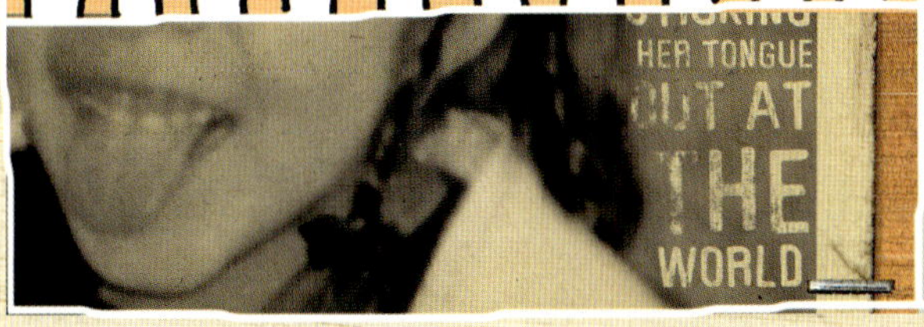

CHAPTER

Seven

Not for the Faint of Heart

Sky diving, *Fear Factor* and watching surgery on the Discovery channel. What do they all have in common? They are all not for the faint of heart. While these pages are not gruesome or life-threatening, they are all a little on-the-edge and showcase the artist's best freestyle work. You'll see a little of this and a little of that and a get a ton of creative inspiration. Whether these ideas stretch your imagination a bit or make your heart skip a beat, they're sure to inspire you to live a little closer to the edge!

63

Autumn
By Tia
Juxtapose color and black and white for a striking layout.

Smile
By Ashley W.
Adhere flashcards to layout to form title. Add random embellishments and findings to complete layout. Use jewelry tags to label items.

On That Day
By Genevieve

Apply artist's gel medium to textured cardstock. Paint with yellow and let dry. Apply brown paint in some areas, then wipe some off using a combination of wet and dry rags, rubbing it into the medium.

Hold Fast
By Genevieve

Adhere patterned paper to a large puzzle piece. Flip it over and cut around the edges with an X-Acto knife. Turn it back over and sand the edges. Add to layout along with photos and patterned paper accents.

Nothing
By Kelli
Adhere found objects to page with adhesive dots to make an "organized collage." Round all edges for more unity.

Applause
By Marilyn
Scribble on cardstock with an orange and red watercolor crayon. Spread color around with a wet brush. Print round photo onto a large piece of textured cardstock. Trim edge into a wave. Adhere to watercolored paper. Stitch randomly, following some of the lines made by the crayons. Stitch onto the left edge of round photo. Print journaling on orange cardstock and trim to the shape of the journaling. Hand cut a scroll pattern from fun foam and use as a stamp.

Elephant Love
By Emily

Cut "windows" in cardstock where photos will be. Glue fabric and ribbon scraps all over cardstock and place on top of another piece of cardstock of the same size. Machine stitch lines to bind together. Attach photos and journaling inside of "frames."

Not So Perfect
By Brenda-Mae

To make flower accent, cut four petals from cardstock. Use a fine-tip pen to draw on the petals. Attach petals together with brads.

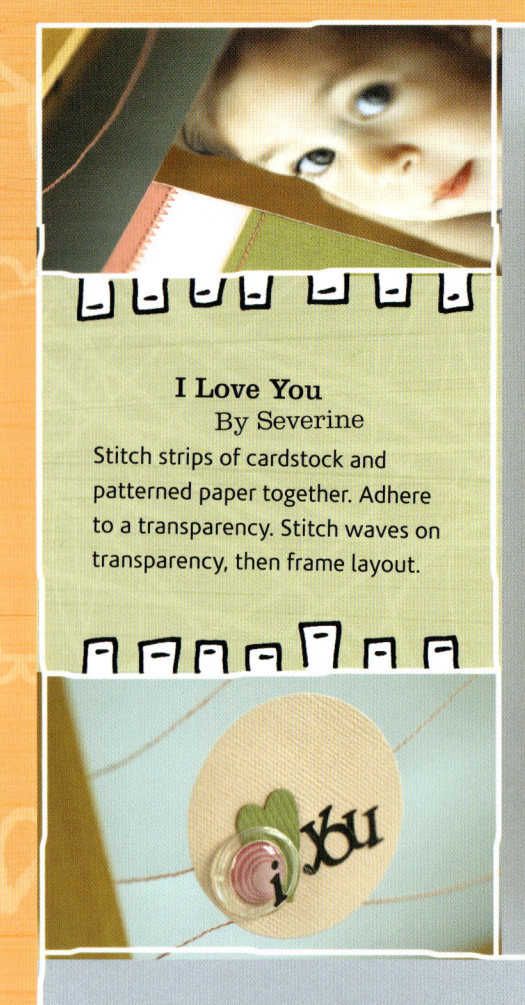

I Love You
By Severine
Stitch strips of cardstock and patterned paper together. Adhere to a transparency. Stitch waves on transparency, then frame layout.

Can You Capture Friendship?
By Emily
Overlap photos to form a collage. Machine stitch lines through bottom pictures. Apply stickers and rub-ons for the title.

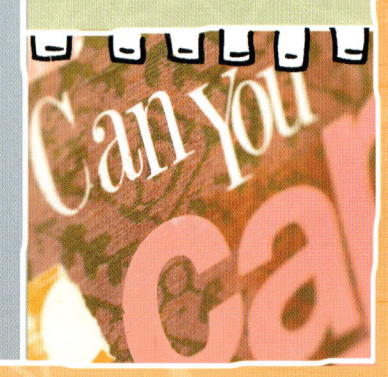

XOXO
By Kim

Stamp on and decorate various sizes of stencils. Set eyelets in the sides of the stencils. Tie stencils together using ribbon, pipe cleaners, netting and string.

Flip Flop
By Tia

To create ribbon shapes, adhere strips of coordinating ribbon to a cardstock background. Machine stitch over the top for interest. Trace desired shapes onto wrong side of cardstock, then cut out. Embellish with hand stitches in the centers.

I love catching a summer time picture of flip-flop clad feet; I originally meant to just grab a shot of my cousins'...but when my kids jumped in with us, the moment was too great to pass up. Can you guess which feet belong to what person? This image is especially symbolic to me, however, since my two cousins don't live on American soil. Seeing all our feet planted on the same ground, if only for a day, makes me happy.

tia**BENNETT**
sara**OAKLEY**
olivia**BENNETT**
hannah**OAKLEY**
braxton**BENNETT**

August 2005

flip-flop**FEVER**

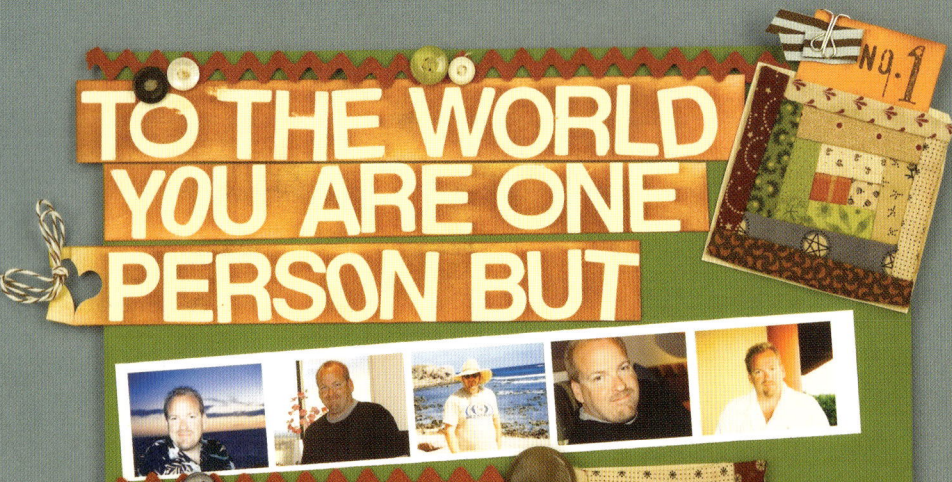

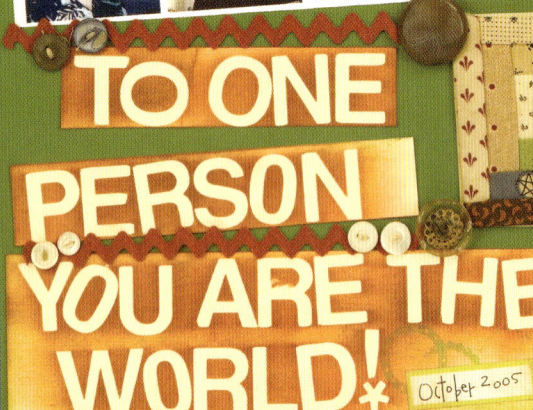

TO THE WORLD YOU ARE ONE PERSON BUT TO ONE PERSON YOU ARE THE WORLD!

The World
By Kim
Make three small log cabin quilt blocks. Place alphabet stickers on cream-colored cardstock. Use sponge to rub stamp ink over stickers, then peel off stickers. Cut journaling into strips and attach to background. Glue photo strip to cardstock. Embellish page with rickrack, buttons and quilt blocks.

Because of Them
By Ashley W.
Staple photo corners onto a photo of blank journal pages. Place a piece of ribbon down the center of the journal. Draw lines, and journal on top. Embellish with a small photo, rub-ons, stickers, tags, flowers and cut-apart title.

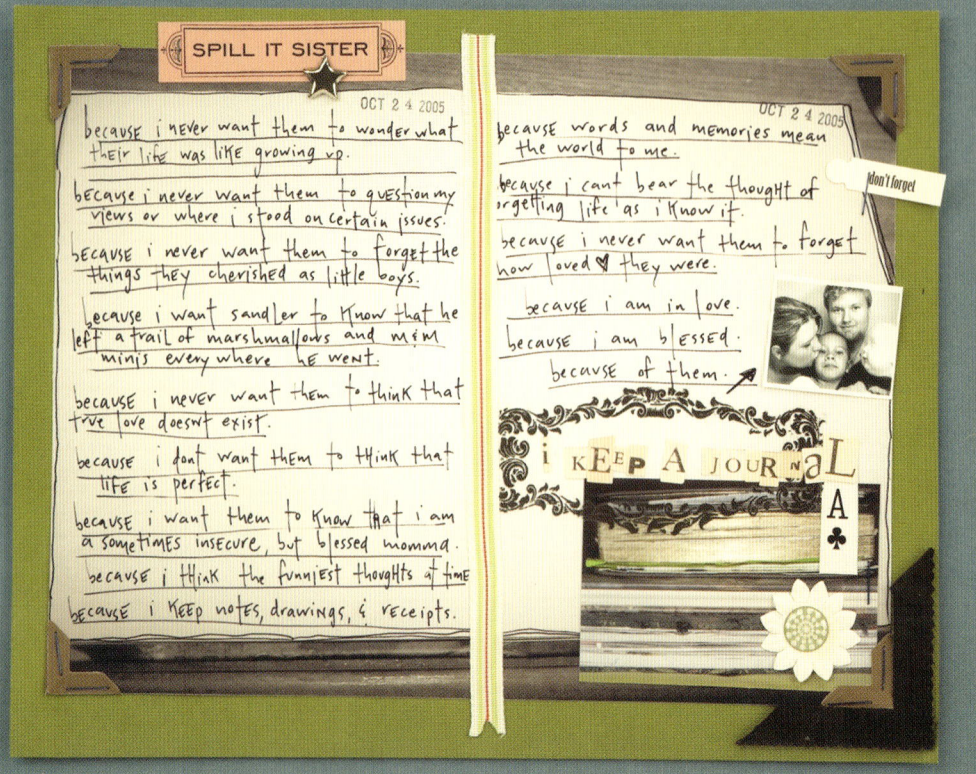

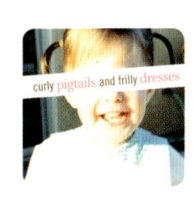

Becoming More Myself
By Chris

Import images into InDesign and arrange on page. Set and tilt titles, subtitles and journaling blocks, then use the Baseline Shift tool to center the paragraph leaders. Add color to key words in layout.

Sisters
By Genevieve

Cut bamboo strips and arrange on page. Add journaling, ribbon and patterned paper in between the strips.

Beauty for Ashes
By Brenda-Mae

To make the fabric flower, cut pieces of fabric into 2" squares. Fold into triangles to make individual petals. Stitch together to make flower. Top with a fabric-covered button.

These Four
By Kelli

Cut flowers from vellum; stitch to page. Adhere library pockets behind each photo and include journaling about each friend.

Practice and Pause
By Danielle

Enhance color in one photo by adjusting the Hue/Saturation and Curves in Photoshop. Adhere to page and surround with colorful buttons. Adhere a black and white photo to the other side along with matching buttons. For more black buttons, back clear buttons with black and white patterned paper.

She is Amber
By Ashley W.

Layer graph paper, polka dot paper and a photo over background. Hand write journaling, then underline with a marker. Add stickers, tabs and flowers as embellishments.

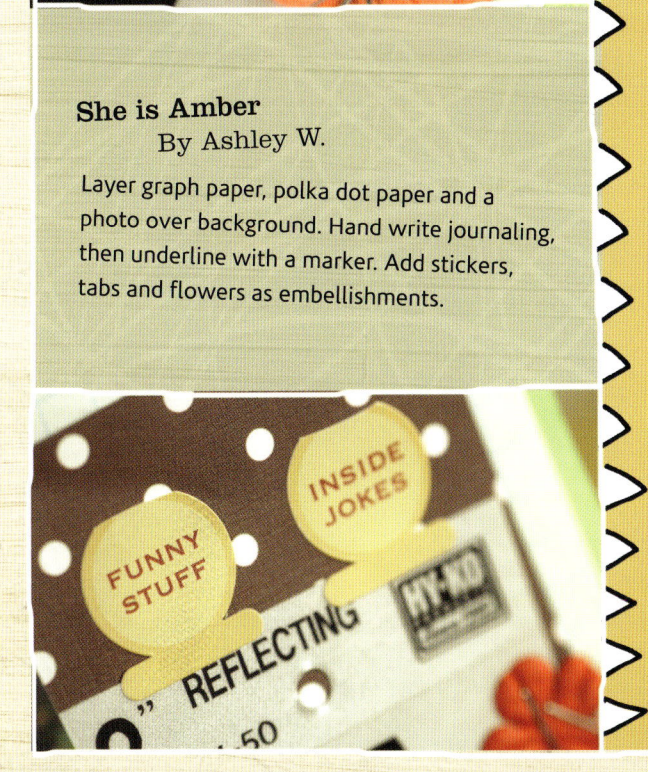

Enchanted
By Linda

Hand cut flower pieces from cardstock and felt. Blanket stitch the edges of the felt flowers with embroidery floss. Layer flower pieces and glue together. Add a button or brad to the center of each flower.

Love at Home
By Ashley W.

Place an enlarged picture in the center of ledger paper. Journal on scraps of ledger paper and cut apart. Adhere to left side. Adhere words cut from a magazine to the right side.

Amazing You
By Linda

Cut hearts from cardstock; embellish with words and buttons. Press each heart into a watermark stamp pad. Sprinkle with embossing enamel, then heat set. While still warm, sprinkle on another layer of embossing enamel. Repeat. Put hearts in freezer for 15 minutes, then remove and bend slightly for a crackle effect. To color twill and fabric, mix one part water to one part paint, then apply with a brush.

Be Glad
By Linda

Attach papers and photos to background. Draw a design to embroider onto the ledger paper. Use watercolor pencils as color for some of the flowers. After embroidery work is done, attach sequins, buttons and star stickers.

Forever
By Severine

Print "FOREVER" on vellum. Hand cut the letters, then attach vellum over a photo with brads.

Perfect
By Jenn

Create the background by cutting varying sizes of old book paper and adhering to chipboard with a gel medium. Coat the paper with white glaze paint.

Hypothesis
By Tia

Use items you'd normally throw away to create this layout. Use negative images of chipboard letters and the actual mask (the black flowers) usually removed from a page.

77

You Make My Heart Full
By Jenn

Cut a heart from cardstock and use a gel medium to adhere the squares over the top. Trim around the edges of the heart. Seal with another coat of gel medium. Stitch buttons around the heart.

Do You Think
By Tia

To use the chalkboard base, draw on the chalkboard with chalk. Spray with a sealer. Attach layout elements over sealed chalkboard.

Cards
By Kelli

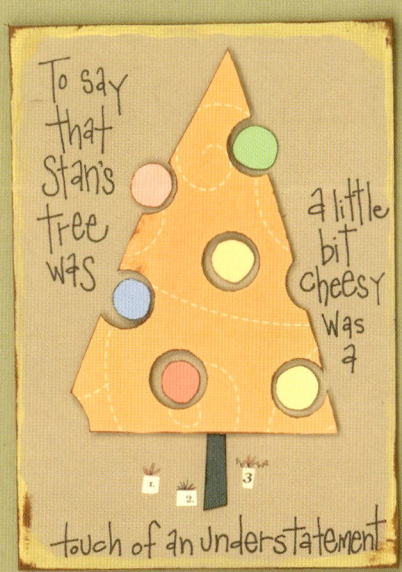

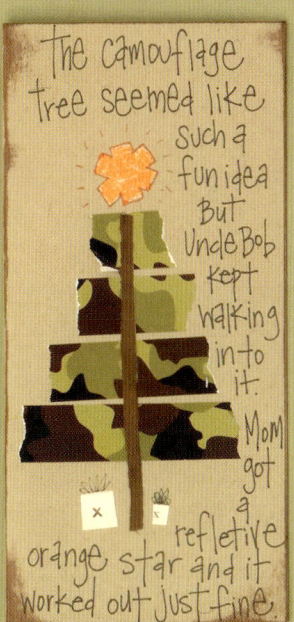

It was really a big box of Love cleverly disguised as a bread machine.

All i want for Christmas is...

To say that Stan's tree was a little bit cheesy was a touch of an understatement.

happy birthday

The camouflage tree seemed like such a fun idea But Uncle Bob kept walking into it. Mom got a reflective orange star and it worked out just fine.

Use patterned paper, fabric, ribbon, tulle and decorative tape to create whimsical designs for the front of humorous cards.

Focus
By Emily
Dry brush acrylic paint onto background cardstock. Sand, then attach chipboard letters. Affix photo and journal in small print all over page.

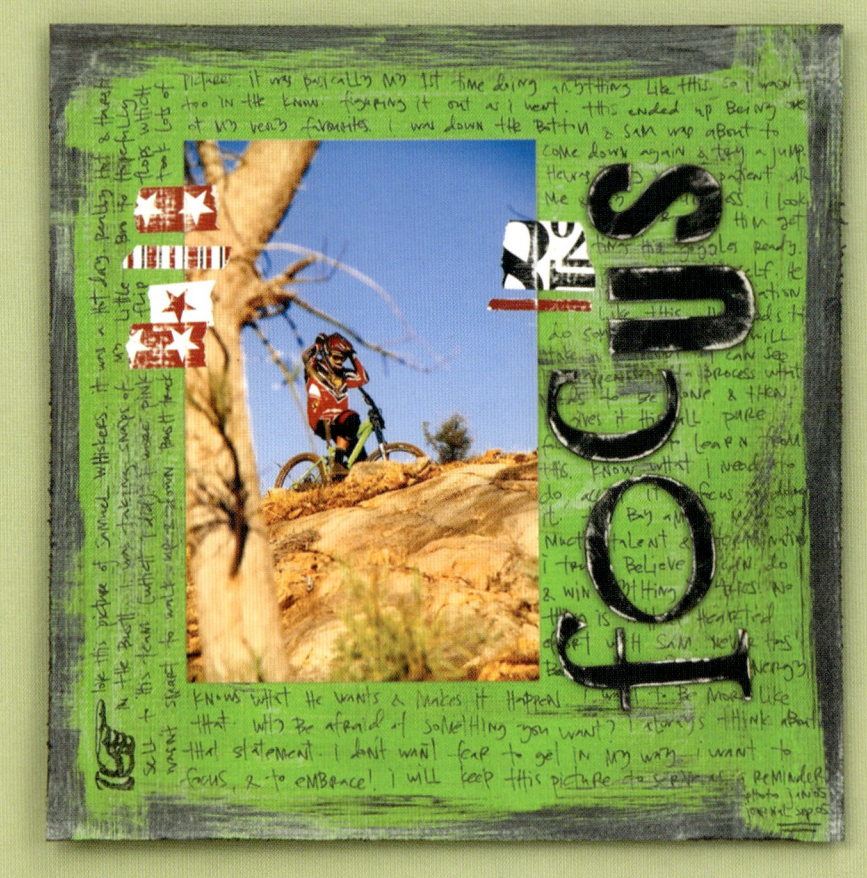

Inspiration
By Kim
With pinking shears, cut several rectangles of fabric and layer on top of each other. Hand stitch in place. Add embellishments over fabric. Place alphabet stickers and flower mask on cardstock. Using a sponge, rub stamping ink over stickers and mask. Remove stickers and mask to reveal title and flower.

Roll
By Brenda-Mae

To make the title ("Roll"), print word in reverse onto cardstock. Cut narrow strips of patterned paper and ink the edges. Glue strips onto right side of cardstock over word. Cut out individual letters.

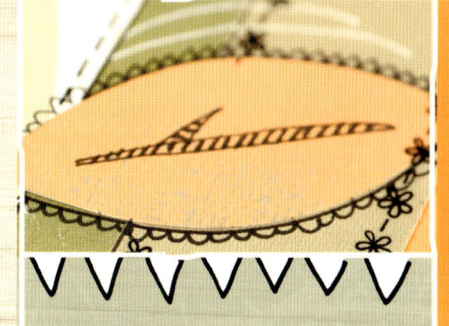

I Thank Heaven
By Tia

Doodle around a photo to create a frame. Doodle lines by objects to reflect "movement," as seen here with the leaves. Journal directly on the photograph.

ID
By Zina
Hand draw title and color in with crayons. Etch an outline with the tip of a ball point pen; cut it out and mat on black cardstock.

Random Silly Moment
By Genevieve
Fray the edges of fabric squares and rectangles. Adhere to page. Stitch a border around the page and around the photo with different colors of thread. Journal on a circle stamped right on the fabric.

82

Bangkok Beauties
By Emily

Create front and back of mini book from two 7½"x6" transparencies. Fold ribbon around the edges and stitch into place. Create 5½"x7" pages for inside. Punch holes through each page and bind with rings. Use acrylic paint and foam stamps to stamp title on cover transparency.

She Becomes
By Emily

Dip a photo in water and remove. Gently sand in all different directions around the edges. Wipe away dust with a wipe. Water down acrylic paint and apply to the sanded area. Wipe away different sections with a wipe. Use a bleach pen to write title and to draw pattern on the photo. Leave on for 10 minutes, then wipe off again with a wipe. Use a photo pen to journal on background.

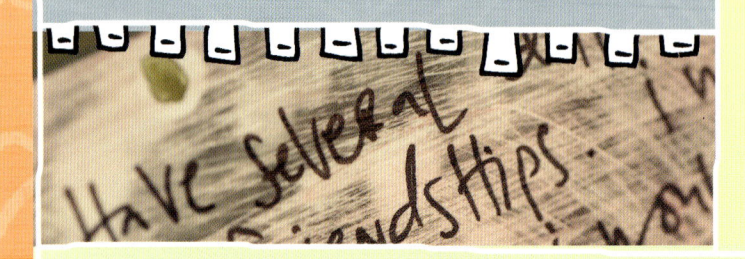

You Amaaaze
By Danielle

Layer stamped shapes and letters for the title; hand draw embellishments with markers and pens.

Spirit Trails
By Linda
Sand playing cards. Using fluid chalk ink, apply color to card surface. Adhere cards to background papers, then machine stitch randomly. Make small holes on some of the cards to "link" together with string.

Jaya & Tali
By Rhonna
In Photoshop, open photo, desaturate and add a sepia filter. On the original photo, desaturate, go to Threshold and adjust the photo until you achieve the look seen here. Create a brush out of this image. Stamp brush on canvas with the color pink. On another layer, stamp in black. Add a Gradient map to the image. Burn, dodge and add doodles and brushes in varying colors, sizes and opacities. To add the type inside photo, click on the large photo with the Magic Wand to highlight the outer edges of the photo. Select Path>Make a Path, then type inside the path with the Type tool.

He's Got Moves
By Danielle

Print black and white photos onto colored cardstock. For the large image, print head onto tan cardstock, then print the costume in color onto photo paper. Layer the costume over the head. Apply rub-ons for the title.

Midnight on the Mediterranean
By Ashley C.

Machine stitch a photo to handmade paper. Sketch swirls on kraft cardstock; cut out with an X-Acto knife. Adhere swirls to layout. Stitch fibers over swirls. Overlap blocks and strips of patterned paper on left side and apply diamond rub-ons. Paint a transparency and layer over paper. Journal on transparency. Set small star nailheads on photo.

Great Oaks
By Chris

Use multiple grunge brushes, Blend Modes and dingbats to create paper flaps. Add photo. Create red band using the Pen tool. Add type and dingbat to strip, then use grunge brushes to add folds and tears. Apply a Drop Shadow to the band to add dimension. Set title, distress using grunge brushes and add a small black stroke.

Love is the Greatest Thing
By Emily

Fingerpaint color onto layout. Use your fingernail to scratch spirals into the paint. Collage paper images onto the background. Attach photo with masking tape. Write and stamp title in ink; wash over the top with gesso to soften.

Products without a credit are either part of the artist's personal stash or not available for purchase.

Note:
Unless otherwise noted, all computer fonts are downloaded from the Internet. 2Peas fonts are downloaded from www.twopeasinabucket.com and CK fonts are from Creating Keepsakes.

Chapter 1
Looks Like an Ad

Hip Little Dude (page 6)
Paper: MM and AL
Gaffer tape: 7gypsies
Acrylic circles: KI
Rub-ons: AL
Font: Great Circus

Geeks in the Future (page 7)
Software: PS
Paper: French Paper Co.
Dingbats: Minipics, Webdings
Transfer: Avery
Fonts: Ed Benguiat and Trade Gothic

Family Picnic (page 7)
Software: PS
Fonts: AL Serenade, C Dans L'air and LHF Mister Kooky
Brushes: Rhonna Farrer, www.twopeasinabucket.com

Why is She Smiling? (page 8)
Paper: Provo Craft
Rub-ons: AL
Bookplate: MM
Font: Angostura

Myopie (page 8)
Paper: CB

Space (page 9)
Paper: Scenic Route
Rub-ons: Heidi Swapp
Fonts: Century Gothic and Downcome

Vintage Chic (page 9)
Paper: AL, Scenic Route and K & Co.
Rub-ons: AL and KI
Photo corners: CB
Stickers: BG
Ribbon: MM
Fonts: Antique Type and Angegardien

06-25-04 (page 10)
Stickers: Hy-ko and Avery
Tag: 7gypsies
Flower: Prima
Stamp: Stampcraft

A Little Push (page 10)
Rub-ons: BG
Stickers: Arctic Frog and Sticker Studio
Tape: Heidi Swapp
Software: PS

My Hope (page 11)
Paper: SEI
Chipboard circle and ribbon: MM
Fonts: Century Gothic and CG PhoenixAmerican

Chapter 2
A Dash of Chaos

This Baby (page 14)
Paper: AL, Wild Asparagus and AC
Photo corner: Heidi Swapp
Ribbon: May Arts
Ink: Ranger
Flower: Prima
Font: Haettenscheweiler

Groucho Max (page 15)
Paper: MM
Stickers: AC
Rub-ons: KI

Their Light Within (page 15)
Paper: AL, Urban Lily, AC and BG
Rub-ons: AL and 7gypsies
Ink: Marvy

Beginner's Mind (page 16)
Paper: CB and SW
Tag: 7gypsies
Ribbon: MM
Photo corner: Heidi Swapp

Pink House (page 16)
Fabric: P&B Textiles
Business card: Paper Source
Rubber stamp: Magenta
Ink: Paper Salon
Twill: AL

I Have This Hat (page 17)
Paper: KI
Ribbon: Li'l Davis Designs

Sabor (page 17)
Frames and slide mount: istockphoto.com
Ink: Ranger
Fonts: Infiltrace Italic, Misproject and Crowns and Coronets

Good Friends (page 18)
Paper: Anna Griffin, CB, Kaleidoscope, MAMBI, AL and AC
Photo corner: Heidi Swapp
Rhinestones: Jo-Ann's
Ink: Ranger
Ribbon: Wrights and Li'l Davis Designs
Font: Fleur Aux Dents

Sand and Sun (page 19)
Paper: Paper Reflections
Stamps: Leave Memories
Ink: All Night Media
Button and stickers: AL

What If (page 19)
Software: PS
Brushes: Rhonna Farrer, www.twopeasinabucket.com
Flowers and stickers: AL and KI
Paper and rub-ons: KI
Stamps: Premo and MM

My Favorite Little Ones (page 20)
Paper: Doodlebug and Paper Source
Fabric: P&B Textiles
Ink: Stewart Superior, Ranger and Paper Salon
Stamps: Postmodern Design

Reach for the Stars (page 21)
Ribbon: Offray
Twill and rub-ons: 7gypsies
Rickrack: Wrights
Belt: Old Navy
Sequins: Westrim
Stamps: Heidi Swapp
Ink: Clearsnap
Stickers: AL

Napa Style (page 21)
Paper: BG
Buttons: AL
Rickrack: MM
Letters: Rusty Pickle

AG (page 22)
Paper: MM
Letters: Li'l Davis Designs
Rub-ons: Doodlebug and AL

Feeling Blessed (page 22)
Paper: BG
Ink: Matisse
Stamp: Inkadinkadoo

I Love You (page 23)
Pillow chips: AL
Ribbon: AC
Gameboard alphabet: MM

10 (page 24)
Paper: KI and Mara-Mi
Rub-ons: AL
Stamp: Purple Onion
Round ringlet: SW

Minnie Kay (page 25)
Paper: KI, Kaleidoscope, AL, AC, Rusty Pickle, Wild Asparagus, Pebbles Inc. and Anna Griffin
Tags: 7gypsies and AL
Photo corners and rub-ons: Heidi Swapp
Ink: Ranger and Tsukineko
Rhinestone: Jo-Ann's
Bottlecap: Li'l Davis Designs

AL Autumn Leaves • **MM** Making Memories • **BG** Basic Grey
SW Scrapworks • **DCWV** Die Cuts With a View • **MAMBI** me and my BIG ideas
AC American Crafts • **CB** Chatterbox • **CI** Creative Imaginations

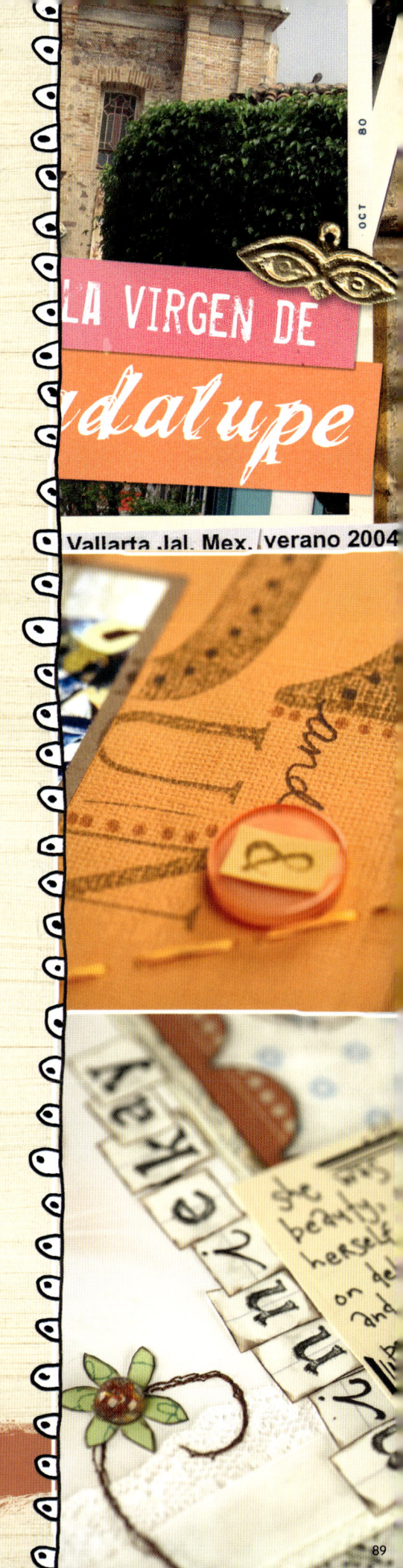

Kaleidoscope *(page 25)*
Paper: Doodlebug
Tag: DMD
Tape: Rainbow Tape and Heidi Swapp
Ink: Stewart Superior and Paper Salon
Label: Russell+Hazel
Stamps: Technique Tuesday
String: Raffit Ribbon

Chapter 3
When One Word Says it All

Wreckage *(page 28)*
Ink: Ranger, Clearsnap and Hero Arts
Stamps: MM
Paper: Mustard Moon

Believe *(page 28)*
Software: PS
Paper and photo edge: Rhonna Farrer, www.twopeasinabucket.com
Fonts and dingbats: New Castle and Apple Garamond

Foundations *(page 29)*
Paper: AL, BG, Karen Foster and CI
Twill and rub-ons: AL
Stamp: CI
Fonts: Old Folks Shuffle and Abadi

Comfort *(page 29)*
Paper: Geneva and Co. and Wild Asparagus

Spooky *(page 30)*
Paper: Provo Craft, KI, Bo Bunny Press and AL
Sticker: KI
Microbeads: Provo Craft

Panic *(page 30)*
Paper: MM, KI, CB, BG, 7gypsies and AL
Ink: Tsukineko
Fonts: Mosh 2, Trixie Plain, AL Fantasy Type and AL Worn Machine

Essence *(page 31)*
Paper: Wild Asparagus, CB and CI
Rub-ons: AL
Twill and ribbon: Carolee's Creations, Remember When and Michaels
Numbers: Walnut Hollow
Font: Another Hand Font, DaFont.com

Brothers *(page 31)*
Paper: SW, 7gypsies, CB, Gin X, Li'l Davis Designs, KI, Karen Foster and MM
Letters: Heidi Grace
Stamps: MM
Ink: Bazzill

Chapter 4
The Artist's Canvas

Turning Five *(page 34)*
Font: Calvin and Hobbes
Buttons: AL

Summer Lily *(page 34)*
Paper: Wild Asparagus, AL, 7gypsies and The Paper Company
Paper frames: Wild Asparagus and CB
Twill: AL
Flowers: Serendipity Designs
Dye: MM
Ribbon: Li'l Davis Designs, May Arts and Wrights
Ink: Ranger, Tsukineko and FiberScraps
Stamps: Ma Vinci's Reliquary
Photo corner: Heidi Swapp

Alex '05 *(page 35)*
Paper: AL and MM
Tape: Heidi Swapp
Rub-ons: MM and AL
Ink: Memories
Stamp: Stampotique Originals

It's All About the Love *(page 36)*
Rub-ons: AL
Paper: Provo Craft
Stamp: MAMBI

He's So Silly *(page 37)*
Paper: AL, Scenic Route, Karen Foster and Urban Lily
Ribbon: MM and SEI
Stickers: AC and Doodlebug
Font: 2Peas Barefoot Professor

Cheerio *(page 37)*
Ribbon: Offray, KI and MM
Rub-ons and buttons: AL
Chipboard letters: Heidi Swapp

Prepare *(page 38)*
Software: PS
Brushes: Rhonna Farrer, www.twopeasinabucket.com
Fonts: AL Songwriter and Cocaine Serif

Pink *(page 39)*
Ribbon: MM
Chipboard heart: Heidi Swapp
Flowers: Prima

Love *(page 39)*
Paper: AC and SW
Photo corners: Heidi Swapp
Fonts: 2Peas Barefoot Professor and 2Peas Fancy Free
Chipboard heart: MM

Friendship *(page 40)*
Rubber cushion: Ma Vinci's Reliquary
Twill: Carolee's Creations
Stickers: EK Success
Pin: MM

Two Guys and a Girl *(page 40)*
Ink: Tsukineko and Clearsnap
Stickers: AC and Arctic Frog
Stamps: Fontwerks

Gamers *(page 41)*
Fonts: Pasteleria and Misprinted Type
Stamp: Fontwerks
Ink: Marvy and Tsukineko

Miss Lilly *(page 41)*
Journaling circle and felt: Paper Source
Fabric: Moda and P&B Textiles
String: Raffit Ribbons
Stamps: PSX
Ink: Paper Salon, Ranger and Tsukineko

Bubby *(page 42)*
Sticker: SW
Rub-ons: MM
Font: Dream Orphan

Fatherhood *(page 42)*
Paper: MM, Deluxe Designs and Christina Re
Ribbon: AL and Li'l Davis Designs
Alphabet and photo corners: Heidi Swapp
Tag: MM
Stamp: Image Tree

Le Petit Monde de Loan *(page 43)*
Fonts: Carpenter, Georgia and Tw Cen MT

Barcelona *(page 43)*
Gel medium: TriArt
Ink: Speedball and FiberScraps
Frame and label: 7gypsies
Tab: AL
Ribbon: May Arts
Wire: Westrim

Heart of a Sutta *(page 44)*
Ink: Speedball
Pin, ribbon and rickrack: MM
Photo corner: Heidi Swapp

Just One Normal Picture *(page 45)*
Rhinestones: Precious Finds
Ink: Memories

Card Set *(page 45)*
Flower and stamp: Heidi Swapp

Chapter 5
Oodles of Doodles

Home *(page 48)*
Paper: AL and KI
Tape: Heidi Swapp
Ribbon: MM

Locks of Love *(page 49)*
Paper: MM and 7gypsies

Doodle Cards *(page 49)*
Paper: 7gypsies, Junkitz and Wild Asparagus
Chipboard: Heidi Swapp
Stickers: AC and MM
Doodle image: Flourish & Dots No. 3, www.designerdigitals.com
Brush: www.designerdigitals.com
Postcard: 7gypsies
Stamp: Fontwerks

Best Friends (page 50)
Paper: CB and Gin-X
Chipboard letter: MM
Photo corners: CB
Ribbon: SEI
Buttons: Michaels

Life in Colour (page 50)
Paper: SW
Pillow chip button: AL
Ribbon: MM

Step Daughter (page 51)
Paper: KI, Gin-X and 7gypsies

Stay True (page 51)
Transparency: AL
Gesso and gel medium: Matisse

Good Times (page 52)
Software: PS
Fonts: Amelie, Apple Scruffs, Rosewood, Circus, Abilene and Designer Mix II

Purpose (page 52)
Letters: MM
Sticker: Hy-Ko
Labels: Li'l Davis Designs
Paper: The Paper Company

This One Picture (page 53)
Paper: The Paper Company
Photo corners: Heidi Swapp
Rub-ons: 7gypsies
Stickers: AL
Flower: Prima

Shoes (page 53)
Software: PS
Paper: KI

Chapter 6
Random Acts of Type

Brown Eyed Girl (page 56)
Software: PS
Brushes: Rhonna Farrer, www.twopeasinabucket.com
Font: AL Scarlet Ribbons

**Completion of the
Sixth Grade** *(page 56)*
Font: Brady Bunch
Label, paper and rub-ons: AL
Milk cap: MAMBI
Watercolor crayons: Lyra
Walnut ink: Postmodern Design
Dyes: MM

Photographer's Paradise *(page 57)*
Paper: Doodlebug and MM
Twill: Paper Source
String: Raffit Ribbons
Ribbon: AC
Muslin: P&B Textiles
Embossing powder: Ranger
Stamp: Postmodern Design
Ink: Tsukineko and Clearsnap
Label: Russell+Hazel
Masking tape: Rainbow Tape
Sponge: AL

Two is Better *(page 57)*
Paper: AL, We R Memory Keepers and KI
Fonts: Century Gothic, Echelon, AL Highlight and Parma-Petit

Heart in Hand *(page 58)*
Paper: AC, BG, AL, KI and Anna Griffin
Photo corners: Heidi Swapp
Sequins: Westrim
Ink: Ranger
Font: Engraver's Hand

Lucky *(page 58)*
Stamps: Heidi Swapp
Ribbon: Offray
Rub-ons: AL
Paper: AL and MM

Kim *(page 59)*
Paper: KI
Button: SEI

Simple Pleasures *(page 59)*
Paper: Doodlebug and KI
Rub-ons: AL, BG and Heidi Swapp
Fonts: AL Messenger, AL Gettysburg, AL Playbook, AL Libretto, AL Scratched, AL Boogie Woogie, AL Highlight, 2Peas Stone Soup, 2Peas Mademoiselle, 2Peas Retro Ways and 2Peas Fat Frog

The Boys *(page 60)*
Paper: 7gypsies, KI and Sweetwater
Tape: Heidi Swapp
Ink: Memories

The Woods *(page 60)*
Tag and bamboo clip: 7gypsies
Ribbon: Michaels
Label sticker: Li'l Davis Designs
Fonts: Hurricane and AL Modern Type

Tomorrow *(page 61)*
Ink: Tsukineko
Rub-ons: Heidi Swapp and AL
Fonts: AL Fantasy Type and AL Worn Machine

I Will Not Change *(page 61)*
Fonts: Keyboard Plaque and Porcelain
Software: PS

Chapter 7
Not for the Faint of Heart

Autumn *(page 64)*
Paper: Junkitz
Chipboard letters: Heidi Swapp and Li'l Davis Designs
Stamps: MM
Tape: Heidi Swapp
Card: Bazzill
Spyglass: Pebbles Inc.

Smile *(page 64)*
Paper: SEI
Frames: CI and MM
Star and flip flops: MAMBI
Photo corners: Heidi Swapp
Rub-ons: AL and 7gypsies
Sticker: 7gypsies and Pebbles Inc.
Index tab and flashcards: 7gypsies
Flower: Prima
Ribbon: Offray

On That Day *(page 65)*
Stamps: MM
Rub-ons: 7gypsies

Hold Fast *(page 65)*
Paper: Provo Craft
Stamp: Fontwerks
Ink: Tsukineko

Nothin (page 66)
Paper: MM
Stickers: AC, 7gypsies, Sticker Studio, MM and Office Max
Labels: Li'l Davis Designs and Pottery Barn
Rub-ons: KI, SW, Li'l Davis Designs and AL
Stamps: Wendi Speciale Designs
Ink: Memories
Number: Li'l Davis Designs

Applause (page 66)
Fun foam: Darice
Stamps: Li'l Davis Designs and Uptown Design
Watercolor crayons: Lyra
Ink: Tsukineko

Elephant Love (page 67)
Rub-ons: AL
Jewels: Heidi Swapp

Not So Perfect (page 67)
Paper: BG
Frame: CB
Ribbon: AL
Font: Dirty Headline

I Love You (page 68)
Frame: IKEA
Paper: CB
Stickers: CI
Epoxy accent: AL
Bubble: KI

Can You Capture Friendship? (page 68)
Paper: Captured Elements
Rub-ons and tape: Heidi Swapp
Stamp: Inkadinkadoo

XOXO (page 69)
Paper: KI, SEI and Treehouse Designs
Cards: Paper Source
Pom-poms and heart: Kaleidoscope
Tape and jewels: Heidi Swapp
Stamps: Rubbernecker Stamp Co., A Muse, JudiKins and Memory Box
Ink: Paper Salon and Ranger
String: Raffit Ribbon
Ribbon: AC and May Arts

Flip Flop (page 69)
Ribbon: May Arts, Doodlebug and KI
Leaves: SW

The World (page 70)
Business cards: Paper Source
Ribbon: AC
String: Raffit Ribbons
Stamps: Hero Arts, Technique Tuesday and Postmodern Design
Label: Russell+Hazel
Ink: Ranger, Paper Salon and Stewart Superior
Embossing powder: Ranger
Sponge: AL

Because of Them (page 70)
Stickers: 7gypsies and AL
Photo corners: Heidi Swapp
Paper: MM and AL
Leather frame and blossom: MM
Ribbon: AC
Rub-ons: AL

Becoming More Myself (page 71)
Software: PS and Adobe InDesign CS2
Fonts: Trade Gothic Extended LH and Cremona

Sisters (page 71)
Paper: Scenic Route, Urban Lily and Anna Griffin
Ink: Tsukineko

Beauty for Ashes (page 72)
Paper: KI and We R Memory Keepers
Rub-ons: Heidi Swapp
Sticker: Marcella
Fabric: Amy Butler
Fonts: Century Gothic, Porcelain and High Tower Text

These Four (page 72)
Paper: The Paper Company
Stickers: AC
Library pockets: Bazzill

Practice and Pause (page 73)
Buttons: AL, Bazzill and 7gypsies
Gaffer tape and twill: 7gypsies
Letters: KI
Rub-ons: AL, Heidi Swapp and 7gypsies

She is Amber *(page 73)*
Letter: Hy-Ko
Flowers: Prima
Paper: CB
Stickers: 7gypsies and Pebbles Inc.
Photo corner: MM

Enchanted *(page 74)*
Paper: CB, BG and Daisy D's
Letters: Mustard Moon, CB and AL
Rhinestone brads: Jo-Ann's

Love at Home *(page 75)*
Paper: MM
Rub-ons: SEI
Heart: Heidi Swapp

Amazing You *(page 75)*
Paper: BG and K & Co.
Stickers: AL, CB and Paper Loft
Twill and fabric strip: Carolee's Creations
Scrabble letters: EK Success
Embossing enamel: Ranger
Ink: Tsukineko

Be Glad *(page 76)*
Paper: BG, Deluxe Designs and MM
Stickers: Wordsworth and Target
Ribbon: May Arts
Sequins: Westrim

Forever *(page 76)*
Paper: AL
Font: Gustavus

Perfect *(page 77)*
Book pages and stamps: Schmootzy
Stamps: Postmodern Design
Stitched embellishments: Li'l Davis Designs

Hypothesis *(page 77)*
Tape, chipboard and mask: Heidi Swapp
Gaffer tape: 7gypsies
Stamps: Fontwerks
Flower: Li'l Davis Designs
Die-cut: SW

You Make my Heart Full *(page 78)*
Paper: KI, Provo Craft, AL, Anna Griffin and Somerset Studio
Buttons: AL
Rub-ons: KI
Acrylic heart: Heidi Swapp

Do You Think? *(page 78)*
Stickers: SW, AC and Li'l Davis Designs
Rub-ons: AL
Flowers: Prima

Cards *(page 79)*
Paper: MM, KI, BG, CB, Anna Griffin, Wild Asparagus and DCWV
Ink: Memories
Stickers: AL
Tape: Heidi Swapp
Rub-ons: Doodlebug
Drawer liner: The Container Store
Ribbon: Jo-Ann's

Focus *(page 80)*
Chipboard letters and tape: Heidi Swapp

Inspiration *(page 80)*
Paper: Paper Source
Pillow buttons: AL
Ribbon: Beaux Regard and May Arts
Stickers: CB and AL
Ink: Stewart Superior

Roll *(page 81)*
Paper: SW and KI
Chipboard circles: MM
Font: Echelon

I Thank Heaven *(page 81)*
Paper: SW
Stickers: Arctic Frog
Rub-ons: AL
Tape: Heidi Swapp

ID *(page 82)*
Paper: AL and KI
Flowers: Heidi Swapp
Pillow chips: AL

Random Silly Moment *(page 82)*
Fabric: Amy Butler
Stickers: AL
Stamp: Heidi Swapp

Bangkok Beauties (page 83)
Stickers: 7gypsies
Stamps: PSX

She Becomes (page 84)
Jewels: Heidi Swapp

You Amaaaze (page 84)
Paper: KI
Stamps: Wendi Speciale Designs, Heidi Swapp, MM, Fontwerks, All Night Media and Impression Obsession
Ink: All Night Media and Clearsnap

Spirit Trails (page 85)
Paper: BG, Anna Griffin and Paper Adventures
Stickers: CB and AC
Washer words: MM
Stamps: MM and CI
Ink: Clearsnap
Playing cards: Hoyle Products

Jaya & Tali (page 85)
Software: PS
Swirl brushes: Rhonna Farrer, www.twopeasinabucket.com
Fonts: 2Peas Sweet Pea and Arriere Garde

He's Got Moves (page 86)
Rub-ons: AL and Marcella
Stamp: Fontwerks
Ink: Clearsnap

Midnight on the Mediterranean (page 86)
Paper: MAMBI, KI, AC and Wild Asparagus
Fibers: CB
Tag: AL
Rub-ons: Heidi Swapp and AL
Ink: Ranger

Great Oaks (page 87)
Fonts: LHFEphemera and LHFTonic
Software: PS

Love is the Greatest Thing (page 87)
Paper: AL
Ink: Matisse and Tsukineko
Stamps: PSX
Tape: Heidi Swapp